TIME FOR CHANGE

NECESSARY CHANGE

via

THE SYSTEM OF NATURE

ROBERT ALMADA

ISBN 978-1-7375102-0-8 (paperback)
ISBN 978-1-7375102-1-5 (eBook)

Printed in the United States of America

Contents

Dedication

—— ✑ ——

This book is dedicated to

My Parents
Ignacio & Emilia Almada

Preface

2020 began with the Coronavirus becoming a worldwide pandemic that has changed the way people interact across the planet. Leaders in states across the US and in countries around the world have contributed to the spread or decline of infections and deaths related to the virus by ignoring science or adhering to scientific and mathematical predictions and suggestions. The questions that have come to the surface as a result of the pandemic are: In the US do we need universal health care? Should there be collaboration between countries to address the problem? Do we have enough supplies to address the problem? Why are communities that live in poverty, primarily black and brown people, affected so much more severely by the virus? Do we need to address our prison population and incarceration policies being as those institutions are severely affected by the virus as well? And what about the homeless? Can we implement changes to address that group of individuals in our society? Even wealth inequality has come to the forefront. Why are the wealthy profiting from the virus? Should there be billionaires in a society? Why is there so much inconsistency in the actions of leaders in the US and the around the world? Due to the pandemic, unemployment has risen to levels that mirror those of the Great Depression. Education has been affected as well. In Illinois, where I live, the governor has followed CDC guidelines. The number of cases in Illinois has steadily decreased. The governor has faced criticism and even law suits but has stayed the course. The numbers support his actions. In states that are ignoring the CDC guidelines the corona virus cases are spiking. Similarly, countries that are not requiring social distancing are also seeing increasing numbers of cases and deaths.

To add to the problems created by the pandemic, recently a police officer in Minneapolis killed a black man by placing his knee on the man's neck so that he could not breath. 8 minutes and 46 seconds later, George Floyd was dead. The incident was recorded and millions of people in the US, and all over the world, watched as yet another person of color was murdered right before our eyes. Protests broke out across the country and around the world. The protest have continued and don't seem to be letting up. The questions that have come to the forefront are: What can we do to eliminate systemic police violence? Should we defund police departments in cities across the country? If so, how do we replace them?

Obviously, we are faced with a multitude of problems. The opportunity is to view this as a time for meaningful changes. I propose that the answers to all the questions we are facing at this critical time in the history of our country and around the world can be found within the System of Nature. What does that mean? Certainly, the vaccine that will stop the corona virus, will only be found within the System of Nature. But does the System of Nature provide cures and solutions to the societal problems we, as a species, are trying to address? I contend that the answer is an unequivocal YES! In this book, I will explain how we can use the System of Nature to address all the problems we experience as a species, as societies, and as individuals.

I begin with an analysis of The System of Nature. Think of this part of the book as The System of Nature 101. We begin with a discussion about the fundamental elements of the System of Nature. We discuss Motion, Individuals, Societies, Truths and Free Will. This discussion will provide an understanding of what the System of Nature is and how it works. I then go into the areas where our society must change. We go over Education, our Justice System, Corporations, Health Care, the roles of Government, and identify changes that must come about in each area as a result of adhering to the System of Nature. This discussion will also include important topics like Income Inequality, Poverty, Endless War, Climate Change and making the world a better place to live for us and future generations.

Chapter I

THE SYSTEM OF NATURE

We deceive ourselves when we abandon experience to believe in imaginary systems. We are created by nature, exist in nature, and adhere to the laws of nature. Even our thoughts are controlled by nature. We cannot escape this reality. Beings that are "above nature" are illusions we have created based on what we have seen and experienced, yet which we can never fully complete with regards to the beings place of existence or it's manner of acting. There can be nothing outside of Nature that includes other beings. Therefore, instead of looking to supreme beings for happiness we should study Nature. We must learn her laws, understand her forces, observe the unchallengeable rules by which she works, and apply them to our existence in order to secure our own happiness. Accept the things in nature that we do not understand as simply that. Know that we are always governed by the laws of nature whether we understand them or not.

MOTION

To understand the System of Nature we start with the fact that everything is in motion at all times. The external motions we experience are easily observed. They are how we learn about the world around us. Internal motion is not as easily seen yet it's effects are undeniable. Beings come into the world and continuously change from the moment of conception to the moment of death. Yes, within the System of Nature, even death can be viewed as nothing more than a change from one state of existence to another. Whether you believe the world we live in came about as a result of an Intelligent Designer or as a result of a Big Bang about 14 billion years ago, the fact that everything from atoms to all other forms of beings that exist on our planet and beyond are in constant motion is undeniable. Laws of attraction and repulsion are always at work on atomic levels, between beings, and even within societies. The laws of nature require all its beings to strive for two outcomes, Survival and Happiness. They drive the existence of all natures creations. We will be looking at how survival and happiness can guide individuals and societies to solve problems and form strong bonds. It is important to note that Nature's laws are immutable and none of her creations have control over her laws. So, when two atoms come into contact they are either attracted to, or repel, each other. These attractions form bonds that in turn form beings, planets and galaxies. To quote Carl Sagan, "We are all made of star stuff!"

INDIVIDUALS

If you believe what we've discussed so far, then you must believe that we, humans, are always striving for survival and happiness. This is true whether a being is born into affluence or poverty. A child who is born into wealth and power will believe that both are essential to survival and happiness. The child born into poverty will seek out happiness and take care of survival needs in very different ways. In both cases, parenting, education, societal norms and infinitely many other factors, form each individuals personality and belief system. Individuals have no control over the circumstances into which they are born. We have no control over the things we are taught to believe. Included are the values and morals that we learn at a young age and that form each individuals personality. Clearly, no two individuals are ever exactly the same. The laws of attraction and repulsion drive individuals toward some and away from others. In striving for survival and happiness, we form bonds with many beings. We form bonds with plants, animals and other humans when they contribute to our survival and happiness. Similarly, we reject connections that appear to threaten one or both. When we bond with enough individuals that identify the need for others, we form a society, and obey laws agreed upon by the majority. We must all play a role in providing for our individual survival and happiness as well as providing for that of others members of the society. We find the most enduring forms of happiness when we help others find a happiness that is right for them.

SOCIETIES

A society is a collection of individuals, all striving for their unique form of survival and happiness. Each individual brings specific skills and products to the society. In doing so, they help others achieve levels of happiness and survival while achieving the same for themselves. A society can be thought of as a being of nature whose survival and happiness are its primary concerns. To address its survival, the members of a society create laws which all members agree to follow. It chooses leaders who promise to represent the interests of the majority. When leaders fail to represent the majority, the people of the society have the right, indeed the obligation, to remove those leaders. When a person or group of people threaten the survival of the society, those people or groups must be trained on how to be a valued member of the society. Such people must be removed until they can be contributing members of the society. In essence, the purpose of incarceration must be focused on re-education and not on punishment. I use the term "re-education" to emphasize that the educational system adopted by a society should teach values that will make all members of the society knowledgeable about the roles each person plays in a nature-based society. The basic ideas must be caring for yourself and your family, as well as helping others in the society find their own forms of happiness. Obvious issues that all societies must address are: education that is truth and nature-based; a justice systems that treats all members of a society as equals; and wealth that is controlled so that all members of the society can achieve happiness. Survival and happiness are the societies promise to each of its members.

TRUTH

The truth will never lead an individual or a society to harm. When we are taught and believe ideas that are not true, the fabric of a good society becomes weak. The morals a society teaches must be based on truth and nature. If we are taught that incarceration is nothing more than punishment, then we believe, and base our actions, on ideas that go against the laws of nature. If we are taught to believe in anything that goes against the laws of Nature, then we base our actions on false beliefs. If a miracle is something for which the laws of Nature must be suspended, then miracles do not exist. Religions and societies are the greatest purveyors of non-truths.

They always do so in an effort to gain power and control over large numbers of people. Whenever leaders or powerful organizations lie for their benefit, they must be controlled by the society within which they exist. Especially when the lies lead to beliefs that result in actions that are harmful to the majority and beneficial to the few. Nature-based truths will always come back to a most fundamental litmus test. Are actions, laws and beliefs based on the survival and happiness of the majority? Of course, since no two people are ever exactly the same, we must acknowledge that there will be a wide range of beliefs and actions that may aide in the survival and happiness of different people. As such, an important concept within a functioning society is to accept that others must live with beliefs different than ours. Truly, the scourge of our species, has been the countless number of lives that have been wasted due to differences in personal, religious, societal and monetary beliefs. The time has come for us to accept our fellow beings.

FREE WILL

There is a debate as to whether we, as individuals, have free will. That is, the ability to make choices regarding our actions. Some have declared the soul to be a free agent. They have given it the ability to move itself and act independent of impulses received from exterior object through organs of the body. They go as far as to say that it can even resist outside impulses and move by its own energies. Yet they insist that it is not different than other beings in nature, it just has a separate mode of action. In other words, it's an isolated point which is not part of the uninterrupted chain of motion whereby bodies communicate to each other in nature and whose parts are always in action. Smitten with their sublime notions, these speculators were not aware that by distinguishing the soul from the body and from all known beings, they make it impossible to form any true idea about it. At this point the body becomes nothing more than a vessel for the soul and the body and soul are unrelated.

This hypothesis leads to questions like, do we have free will regarding the situations into which we were born? Do we have control over the things we were taught and exposed to in our early years of development. Most will agree that these are areas in which we have no say. If you agree, at what point does free will kick in for humans? Many religions identify an "Age of Reason" at which time we have free will, are accountable for all our actions, and can be rewarded or punished for those actions. Similarly, societies declare an age at which an individual can be held accountable for actions. Both organizations promise consequences for actions that go against their teachings, either after death or more immediately. These teachings and beliefs are lies that go against the laws of Nature. They are taught in hopes of frightening and controlling large groups of people.

The question occurs, if there is no free will, that is if all our actions are determined by an infinity of causes that our brains have experienced since conception, then can we hold anyone accountable for their actions? We can and we must. We do so by creating consequences for actions. When actions are harmful to individuals and/or the society in which we live, the society must respond.

When an individual makes a choice, that leads us to believe we have free will. In reality, that choice is the result of countless experiences, most of which are instilled in us at a very young age and which we had no control over receiving. Those experiences form our personality and our temperament. Recall that the driving forces of Nature are survival and happiness. Most people, who are well adjusted, will respond to consequences that threaten their chances for survival and happiness. Their response is not an act of free will, but a function of the persons temperament. The person who is not well adjusted and continues to threaten the well-being of members of the society, must be controlled and re-educated until that person can be a contributing member of the society in which he or she lives. Nature demands that all beings, of which a society is one, strive for survival and happiness. Free will is a myth created by evil beings who strive to control others. Such people have no free will in their actions and are a necessary part of the System of Nature, which creates good and evil without forethought or malice. We are here as a result of an infinite number of causes and effects that we had no control over, as is the planet we live on, the solar system we are part of, and the countless galaxies of which we are aware.

If all of our lives are a straight line from birth to death then what is the point of life? The immediate answer is survival and happiness for ourselves and others in the moment in which we are living. By understanding the truth of our existence, we must work diligently to educate our children about nature-based truths so that future generations will know the importance of treating all members of their societies with dignity and respect. This is how societies, which are beings of nature, will continue to survive and become strong. As individual beings that are part of a bigger whole, we are the catalyst for the necessary changes that will make our society a place where all members can survive and be happy.

Chapter II

EDUCATION

The most fundamental idea in creating a well informed citizenry is that of Education. A Nature based education system begins with teaching truths. Since education begins with parenting, it is important that a society attempts to make sure there is a consensus regarding the truths we teach our children. I know this is a tall order, yet it is up to the society to work to instill fundamental truths in all of its members. The most basic truth is that we must feel a sense of self worth. The earlier this truth is instilled and nourished within young people, the better. Yet another truth is that we experience true happiness when we find ways to make others happy. The ideas of self respect and helping others are the foundations needed to build a strong society. These ideals must be re-enforced at every level of the educational system.

Cultural and religious beliefs are taught by parents and schools within a society. But what if those beliefs teach ideas that are based in superstitions instead of truths. The society must devise a nature-based curriculum and share it with all members of the society. Although the society cannot force private schools and parents to adopt a nature-based philosophy and curriculum it is important to inform members of the society. If all schools are teaching the importance of accepting others regardless of race, religion, skin color or social status, you will have an advanced and productive society. When institutions or individuals go against the acceptance of others based on different beliefs, they must be addressed since they can be destructive to the society as a whole.

FREE EDUCATION

Did you know that college debt has overtaken credit card debt within the United State? Currently, graduating from college is not only an accomplishment but a life sentence. A society that sees the value of educated members who can solve problems and contribute to the well being of the majority, will always treat education as a right. Such a society will go to extremes to make sure that all its members have access to, and receive, a quality education. Funding education from preschool to advanced degrees will pay dividends back to the society as a whole in many ways. One of the biggest detriments to education in the US are privatized schools. These schools look to profit from education while controlling the curriculum. They widen the gap between the very poor and the very wealthy. In many cases their teachings are outright lies that re-enforce stereo-types and go directly against Nature-based education and science. Free Nature-based education must be viewed as a human right.

Some ask the question, "How will we pay for such an initiative?" This question is not only asked about free education, but also with regards to ending poverty, homelessness and hunger, and addressing many other societal needs. The most obvious answer is to defund our military. We spend more on our military than the next 10 or 11 countries combined. War benefits only the companies that profit from that industry. It is a crime against humanity to profit from war at the expense of our society, other societies and mankind. Another solution is to defund police and replace them with social agencies within each community. Yet another solution is to fairly tax the most wealthy in the society.

CHALLENGES

The biggest challenges to providing a quality education to all members of a society are being able to identify truths and lies for what they are. So much of what we teach our children works to confuse them, and is sometimes meant to deceive them. Religious dogma is a major source of lies and confusion. Teaching children that there is a place where they go after death that might include eternal suffering is just downright cruel. Teaching young minds that they are born with sin, and will only be happy after they are dead, is ridiculous. Once again, we must look to Nature for the truths that will set us free and make teaching natural truths the focus of our educational systems.

Yet another major challenge is making sure all schools are teaching a Nature based curriculum. It should not matter if a school is in the city or in the suburbs. This is more of a funding issue that must be addressed. The elimination of poverty and slums is central to addressing this aspect of education.

Eliminating college debt is another challenge that must be addressed. Young people come out of college with debt that will last a lifetime. Once again this is more about making the rich more wealthy while strapping the poor and middle class with a lifetime of debt. This is how the very wealthy keep their money while making it almost impossible for poor and middle class families to move up in the society. We live in a society to protect us from this kind of tyranny. Free education is an essential part of a Nature-based society.

Reason and morals are useless if they do not point out to each individual that one's conduct is beneficial only if it helps ones-self and others. For a person's conduct to be useful it must help the individual gain the favor of the beings that are necessary for personal happiness. So, in the interest of mankind, which is for the happiness of the human race, early education should teach the importance of self-esteem, love for fellow beings, and the advantages of both. Education should positively stimulate the imagination of each citizen. This is the true means of getting those happy results that habits will make familiar, that public opinion will honor, and that example will continuously direct us toward.

Chapter III

∝

LAW AND ORDER

*P*olitics has repeatedly adopted wrong opinions based on ideas that are not capable of satisfying the passions that everything conspires to kindle in the heart. From all this, it is obvious what is necessary to lead us to happiness and how error provides obstacles to oppose it. The system of Nature creates good and evil without malice or forethought. When survival and happiness of individuals or the whole of society are threatened, Nature requires action for its preservation. As such, Judicial Systems, Police, and Jails are necessary parts of a society.

JUSTICE

A Nature-based system of justice will know that there is no free will and a persons actions at any moment are determined by infinitely many causes and effects. As such, the severity of a persons actions, how much of a threat they present to individuals and the societies, must be taken into account. A reasonable person will always respond to consequences in a positive manner. The person who is not well adjusted must be treated differently. Within a Nature-based justice system there must be a way to assess the mindset of a perpetrator. In a true system of justice, the punishment always fits the crime. In a flawed system of justice, criminals do as they wish while innocent people are stifled and even put in jail. A sure sign that the society has lost its way is when people who are contributing members of the society are locked up while the evil and powerful are never prosecuted. In the US we have a two-tiered justice system. One for the wealthy and powerful and one for everyone else. When the system of justice is not working for the good of society, then the people must be the catalyst for change.

POLICE

Nature-based policing requires that police be well trained as communicators. Their jobs are to deescalate situations and send people on their way. Force should only be used when absolutely necessary. Unfortunately, at this time in our country, police have a shoot first ask questions later mentality. The execution of George Floyd by a police officer in Minneapolis has started protests that have spread across the country and around the world. Many cities are demanding the defunding of their police departments and moving that money to fund citywide services to address schools, poverty, homelessness, the mentally ill and so much more. Most situations require trained professional without guns, who are experts in dealing with the different aspects of citizens in a society. Currently, many situations end up in violence because instead of calling a social worker, we call an armed police officer. If your only tool is a hammer, all your problems will begin to look like nails.

In many cities candidates for police work are turned away if they are too empathetic or intelligent. Then, in training, it is affirmed that

13

they are going into a violent job that requires the use of superior violence. Is it any wonder our police are killing people, mostly of color, at an alarming rate? It is a fact that police in the US started out as armed slave patrols. Hunting and killing people of color was just part of the job. It certainly appears that not much has changed over the last 200 years. As a society, our truth is that our country was built on the backs of slaves and genocide. The time has come for us to acknowledge our wrong doings and make the necessary changes.

JAILS

There are so many wicked and vicious people on this planet because there are so few governments that make people feel the advantages of being just, honest, and happy. Instead, in most places, the interest of the powerful invite the common citizens to criminal behavior by favoring the inclinations of a vicious government and by tolerating desires which nothing has tried to control or lead to virtue.

We must have a place to re-educate and rehabilitate the members of society who threaten the safety and happiness of individuals and the society as a whole. I cannot stress enough that the focus of taking people out of the society must be rehabilitation and not punishment. So, instead of jails, we should have schools and facilities that are run by organizations that specialize in re-educating offenders until they can fit back into the society and be contributing members. Right now many of our jails are run by private organizations and are a source of profit for big companies. The more inmates the better for the bottom line of these organizations. Is it any wonder that we incarcerate more people, mostly of color, than any other country on the planet? This must change if we are to have a Nature-based society.

The only solution is for the government to oversee the re-education and rehabilitation of people who need to be removed from the society.

One of the biggest factors contributing to the incarceration of so many people of color is "The War on Drugs." It is no secret that this initiative was put in place to put people of color in jail for minor offenses related to the use of marijuana. The time has come to release non violent offenders. The real criminals are the CEO's and leaders who crash economies, pollute, create wars, charge too much for sickness and pharmaceuticals, and charge too much for college loans, all for their profit. These are the sociopaths that a good society will put into a jail for re-education. If they see there are consequences for actions that are detrimental to the society, they will change or stay in re-education.

For the unfortunate beings that live in continuous contradiction with themselves, never finding inner peace or the ability to conform within a society, whatever your crimes and whatever your fears of punishments in another life are, aren't you already cruelly punished in this life? Don't your own excesses and shameful habits result in poor health, disgust, and fatigue? Don't your vices dig your grave as you live everyday with the knowledge of your actions? Don't you tremble with the fear that you may be caught, or worse that you have to see a person with so many problems every time you look in the mirror? You should not fear death as it will put an end to the torments you have inflicted on yourself. Death, in delivering from the earth a troublesome birth, will also deliver you from your most cruel enemy, yourself.

Chapter IV

⌘

CORPORATIONS

In a Nature-based society, businesses provide essential services that contribute to the survival and happiness of most members of the society. Unfortunately, in the US, capitalism is completely out of control. Many large companies are only concerned with making profits at all costs. Instead of serving the communities in which they exist, they serve their top administrators and their board of directors. This is a flaw in the system that can be addressed. First, if a company does not clearly show that it is working to serve the community, it must have its license to operate revoked. This has been referred to as the corporate death penalty. Secondly, the board of directors for all corporations must consist of an equal number of employees and administrators. In this kind of corporation decisions regarding pay and working conditions would benefit all employees and not just the people at the top. Another way to accomplish this end is for a business to be formed as a co-operative. That is, where all employees are owners and decision makers. Yet another form of democracy in the work place is the existence of unions. Unions should work with management to make sure that all sides are getting a fair shake while serving the community. The rap on Unions is that they have too much power. This is a narrative pushed by the corporate media to build sentiments against unions. The solution is that unions and corporations must be formed to serve the societies within which they exist. Their formation must consist of a Vision, a Mission and Core Values that declare their commitment to serving the society in which they exist. Small and large businesses must be committed to working toward the survival and happiness of their society, their employees and their administrators.

Chapter V

HEALTH CARE

In the US health care is a for profit business. As such many Americans don't have sufficient coverage or have no coverage at all. For many Americans a hospital visit or extended sickness results in debt that lasts a lifetime. The cost of pharmaceuticals is a for profit business as well. In the US we pay exponentially more for the life-saving drugs we need. Our choice is pay or die. This is no choice at all. A Nature-based society identifies health care as a human right. At that point the society steps in to assure all its members get the care they need, when they need it, at no cost. Look around the world and, in most advanced countries, you will see health care that puts that of the US to shame. With the Covid 19 pandemic ravaging our country, we have the most cases and deaths on the planet, the need for free health care for all has come to the forefront.

One does not have to look beyond our borders for examples of where free health care is working just fine. The military is a prime example of free health care for all, at least while you are serving. That system has been deteriorated by the withdrawal of funding so that when soldiers return from active duty, they are left with next to nothing.

Many become homeless and the suicide rate for this group is much higher than the national average. On the other end of the spectrum we see public officials receive the highest quality health care for life.

To strive for the survival and happiness of all its members, free health care is an important ingredient. It is another idea whose time has come.

Chapter VI

─────────── ❧ ───────────

GOVERNMENT

I n a Nature-based society the government will address and enforce solutions to all of the above. Unfortunately, our elected officials are frequently beholding to businesses, wealthy individuals, and powerful lobbies. All must be eliminated from Washington and their ability to influence our politicians and our elections. Currently, laws are passed that give the wealthy unlimited power with no consequences for their actions. In many cases, such people and businesses pay no taxes and have no obligation to serve our society. These groups want us to believe that government power is a bad thing, yet they wield unlimited power. The solution is that the government and businesses that exist within the society must declare their focus and commitment to serving society and not the wealthy. It is the governments job to oversee that no one breaks the laws set forth by the society.

Ultimately, it is we the people who oversee the actions of our leaders. Those leaders must be accountable for their actions and removed from office when they fail to meet their obligations to the society. The best place to take such action is when voting. However, if the system has been corrupted and the elections have been rigged, other actions may be necessary. The current outcry for changes at all levels of our society is a sign that the time for change is upon us.

Government should recognize those who follow the plan and re-educate those who interrupt it. The hope of true welfare and the fear of undesired consequences will be passions strong enough to deter those that might be harmful to society. Such people will be rare when, instead of feeding our mind with unintelligible speculations and words that make no sense, we are taught only realities and shown only those things that are in unison with truth.

Chapter VII

SOLUTIONS THE GOVERNMENT
MUST OVERSEE

MONEY

Get money out of politics. Politicians should only be beholding to their constituency and not their donors. Billionaires should not be allowed to exist within any society, let alone influence elections and buy politicians. The more money one has, the more one should be taxed. If you were a business owner who had to choose between putting money back into your business by paying better wages or hiring more people, or give that money to the government in the form of taxes, what would you do? Within a well run government, tax revenue would help address issues like education, health care, income inequality, poverty, social programs, housing and so much more.

VOTING

Voting is supposed to give the people of a society the feeling that they can make a difference by participating in the selection of leaders. Unfortunately, the choices we are given in our two-party system are owned by the wealthy and do not represent the majority. It's a system of voting where the winner takes all, but does not require a majority of the votes. It is a flawed system created by the wealthy to protect their interest. Another part of that system is the Electoral College. After the Civil War, it was used as an incentive to give Southern states a stronger say in controlling our elections while at the same time giving the very wealthy the ability to control election results. It limits the voice of the poor and middle class. How many times has a candidate lost the presidency due to the Electoral College while winning a majority of the votes. Al Gore and Hillary Clinton come to mind. Strategist on both sides of the aisle plan campaigns around the Electoral College when considering advertisements, voter disenfranchisement strategies, gerrymandering, and so much more to ensure their candidates success. The solution is to get rid of the two party system and replace it with Rank-Choice Voting. Maine is the first state to implement this kind of voting. In Rank-Choice Voting there can be as many candidates as the system will permit, and the winner must get a majority of the votes. Also, we need to make voting accessible to all members of the society by allowing for voting by mail, voting in person, and making voting day or weekend a holiday.

EDUCATION

Education is the springboard for meaningful and lasting systemic changes. First we must base instruction on natural truths. The most important of these truths are respect for ones self and for others. It must be ingrained in our students and all members of the society that we can only realize true happiness by making others happy. A second major idea of Nature-based education is that we are all different, yet it is of the utmost importance to accept all members of the society regardless of race, religions, cultures and skin color.

A major problem in the US is the cost of getting a College Degree and an Advanced Degree. Financial institutions and collection agencies make college education a for-profit industry. College at every level must be free.

The society must create a truth-based curriculum that can serve as a guide to all educational institutions and parents. Communication between the societal government and the educational institutions is a must so each knows what the other is teaching.

POLICE

Currently our police are trained to kill, weaponized for war, and have no accountability for their actions. Police unions go to bat for their members with no accountability to the community.

Poorly formed unions represent only their members and forget about a commitment to the community. Unions that forget or ignore this part of their commitment to the society must be disbanded. Police unions have fought for and acquired Qualified Immunity for its members. This means that police cannot be held accountable for their actions in most situations, including murder.

It is also okay for police to keep their records of past actions confidential. This gives officers the ability to commit wrong doings and have no record of their actions. In this way they can move to another city and repeat the same offenses again and again. A national database must be created to hold all law enforcement officers accountable for their actions and remove them when necessary. Yet another systemic problem is that District Attorneys, who frequently work closely with police departments, fail to bring charges against and prosecute police officers who have committed crimes of murder, assault and other serious infractions. For these situations outside prosecutors must be brought in to make sure all trials and prosecutions are fair.

We must train our police to deescalate situations and resort to force only when absolutely necessary. Police departments must be replaced with social programs that address situations that present no danger to others. Qualified Immunity and Confidential Records, which make police unaccountable and untouchable for their misconducts, must be eliminated. Police unions must be required to serve the community first or be disbanded. It has never been more clear that now is the time to reform policing in America.

JUSTICE

A Nature-based justice system believes that people have no choices yet must be controlled if they cause harm. Removing individuals from society must be to re-educate them so they can return to society. Punishment should never be a motive. Sentencing of offenders must always fit the offense.

CORPORATIONS

Corporate Charters must declare how the corporations will contribute to society. The government will hold them accountable and subject them to the corporate death penalty, disband them, if they fail to comply with the terms of their Charter. The board of directors must consist equally of workers and managers. Cooperatives and unions are also solutions to help end corporate power, greed and control over our politicians.

HEALTH CARE

Free health care for all must be recognized as a human right and enforced by the government. Medicare for all is the solution whose time has come. The pharmaceutic industry and medical insurance companies must be regulated or disbanded by the government.

WAR

The current situation in the US is that war is profitable for the very wealthy and destructive to everyone else. We spend more money on our military than the next ten countries combined. We can end hunger and poverty in our country and around the world by diverting half of our military budget toward social causes. Indeed many of the aforementioned issues can be addressed with the money we spend on wars.

In a well formed society it will be against the law to profit from war. Businesses that operate with war as a main source of income must be eliminated. The NRA is an organization that wields far too much power in our country and on our politicians. They are responsible for the mass shooting that have ravaged our country. Incorporating background checks and eliminating the sale of assault weapons is a start.

CLIMATE CHANGE

Within Nature we will find the solutions to all of our toughest problems. We must look to science for answers to climate change, Covid 19 and unknown future problems. We must work together, as a society, as a country, and as a planet to find the Nature-based solutions to all the problems we face.

A government that is equitable and vigilant will fill a society with honest citizens by showing them reasons for goodness, the advantages of truth, and real motives to be virtuous. By instructing people in their duties and fostering them with its goals, government will allure us with the promise of happiness for each individual.

Chapter VIII

⸺ ❧ ⸺

ERRORS, HAPPINESS & EVIL

Reason does not stop us from having big desires. Ambition is a useful passion when it is applied to obtaining the happiness of mankind. Great minds and elevated souls always want to extend their sphere of influence. Powerful geniuses, enlightened beings, and philanthropic people must spread their caring influence in order to make themselves happy while making countless others happy. So many people of wealth and power fail to enjoy true happiness because their feeble and narrow souls must act in a sphere too large for their energies. So, due to the laziness, passiveness, and ineffectiveness of leaders, nations frequently pine in misery, ruled by little minds that can't determine their own happiness let alone that of the people they govern. On the other hand, those leaders who are controlled by their passions are tormented by the narrow sphere that they live within and their aggression becomes a curse to the human race. Rulers on either side of this unfortunate coin are never in tune with their sphere of action.

Our happiness will always be a function of the harmony that exists between our desires and our circumstance. The power an individual leader possesses means nothing if it cannot be applied to the advantage of the governed which in turn would bring about the happiness of the leader. If the actions of the powerful are truly evil those actions make them miserable, and if they produce misfortune for some portion of the human race then such actions are detestable abuses. Most leaders don't know happiness. The people they rule are unfortunate because bad leaders focus on making themselves content without caring about citizens or because all they know about the general population are their response to abuse. A wise leader would be the happiest of mortals. The leader who is hated yet maintains an advantage over the population through subjugation, and whatever other unscrupulous methods are created to occupy a deprived mind, is the saddest of all individuals. The virtuous leader with an expansive mind uses power to gently unite and kindly consolidate the wills of authority with the wills of the governed. Respect, affection, and a positive place in the pages of history are earned through such actions. These are the conquests that reason offers to all who are destined to lead empires. Such conquests are grand enough to satisfy the most active imaginations yet sublime enough to please the largest ambition. Evil leaders see them as duties that must be fulfilled while true leaders are the happiest of individuals because they use their ambitions to make others happy which in turn brings happiness to them.

Riches, which can be harmful to many, in the hands of an honest individual can provide countless ways of enhancing happiness. But, before wishing for wealth one should know how to use it. Money is only a symbol of happiness. To enjoy it one must use it to make others happy. This is the great secret; the jewel; the reality! Money allows us to purchase those things which we desire yet the only thing it will not buy is *the knowledge of how to use it properly*. To have money without the knowledge of how to enjoy it is like having the key to a mansion that we are prohibited from entering. If we try to go inside we cause harm to ourselves and others. If we are enlightened with a sound mind and an extensive soul we will not be overwhelmed by wealth and power. Instead our benevolence will shine through earning us the respect, love, and praise of all who are within our sphere of influence. We will know that restraint is the only way to truly enjoy the pleasures we experience. We will know that all the treasures in the world cannot renew the mind, body, and soul, in short the senses, when they have been worn down by excess.

The right a human being has to rule over fellow beings can only be founded on the actual happiness secured for them or the promise of future happiness. Without real or promised happiness, the power exercised is violence, occupation, and manifest tyranny. Legitimate authority must be based on its ability to make others happy, without which it's nothing more than the *baseless fabric of a vision. No individual derives from nature the right of commanding another.* But it is voluntarily given to some by the masses with the expectation of their welfare as a result. *Government* is the right of commanding given to leaders specifically for the advantages of the governed. Political leaders should be defenders of the people, protectors of property, and guardians of the liberty of their subjects. In return the people consent to obey the laws set forth by the governors. Government becomes nothing more than a robber when it uses the powers given to it by the people to make society unhappy. *The empire of religion* is founded on the idea that it has the power to make nations happy. Government and religion are reasonable institutions, but only to the extent that they contribute to the felicity of the human race. It would be silly to submit to a yoke that results in nothing but evil and misery. It would be complete injustice to force us to renounce our rights without some corresponding advantage!

The happiness we experience is the invariable and necessary standard for how we judge the people with whom we associate, the objects we desire, the opinions we embrace, and our actions. We fall victim to our prejudices every time something other than this standard guides our judgment. We will never deceive ourselves if we look closely at how religion, superstition, laws, institutions, inventions, and the various actions of all mankind affect our species. And if we are seduced by a superficial promise of happiness, experience aided by reflection will guide us back to reason which will never deceive. We will learn that pleasure is momentary happiness which frequently becomes an evil, and that evil is temporary trouble that frequently becomes a good. We grow to understand the true nature of objects which enable us to foresee the effects we should expect. We become capable of distinguishing between the desires that are beneficial to our welfare and those seductions that we should resist. We will be convinced that the true interests of intelligent beings who love happiness and want to live in that mode is to root out all phantoms, eliminate superstitious ideas, and destroy all prejudices that denigrate virtue and obstruct happiness in this world.

If we look to experience we will see that illusions and false opinions which have become sacred over time are the source of many evils which overwhelm mankind almost everywhere. Due to our ignorance of natural causes we create imaginary causes. When we do not understand how something works or why some things happen we resort to faith in imaginary beings. The threat of eternal punishment makes these imaginary causes fatal ideas that haunt us without making us better people. We tremble without benefit to ourselves or others. Our minds are filled with superstitious ideas that defy reason and prevent us from seeking after our own happiness. Our fears make us slaves to those who deceive us under the pretense

31

of caring about our welfare. We commit acts of evil because we are persuaded that our Gods demand sacrifices. We live in poverty because we are taught that these Gods want us to be miserable in this life. We become slaves to beings created by our own imagination and we never dare to break the chains that bind us. The artful priest and ministers of these divinities lead us to believe that stupidity, the renunciation of reason, idleness of the mind, and despair of the soul, are the surest means of obtaining eternal happiness.

In many cases nations are ignorant of the true foundations of authority. And out of fear or ignorance or both people dare not demand happiness from those leaders whose job it is to procure it for them. As a consequence, politics almost everywhere has degenerated into the fatal art of sacrificing the interests of the majority and providing for those of a few privileged irrational beings. In spite of the evils that assault them, nations follow the leaders they have allowed to rule them, foolishly respecting the instruments of their misery. They show a stupid veneration for those who continuously injure them, obeying their unjust will, giving their blood, money, and lives to satisfy the never ending wants of these leaders. They put their happiness in the hands of individuals who, due to their vices and lack of virtue, are not capable of making themselves happy. Under such leadership the physical and moral happiness of the majority are neglected or even annihilated.

Superstition, which never had anything but ignorance as its foundation and a chaotic imagination as its guide, does not base ethics on our nature or our relationships or the duties that come about as a result of our relations. Instead, in unison with itself, it bases ethics on imaginary relationships which it pretends exist between humans and the invisible powers it so gratuitously imagines. So, superstition, instead of providing a sure and natural basis for morals gives a shaky foundation at best by demanding ideal duties and acceptance of ideas which are impossible to accurately understand. In other words, superstition first corrupted us, and then penances performed to atone for our actions finished the job by ruining us. When superstition tries to combat our unruly passions it is unsuccessful. Always enthusiastic but lacking experience it has no clue about true solutions. Those it passes as divine remedies are disgusting and only suitable to make people revolt against them. They are ineffective because fantasies cannot control our basic passions to which more real and powerful motives give birth and our nature constantly move us toward. The voice of superstition, or the Gods, could not be heard amidst the confusion of society. Still the religious leaders cry out to us that we cannot be happy without injuring our fellow beings, who are at fault for having different opinions. These vain cries make virtue hateful because it is viewed as an enemy to happiness and the curse of human pleasure. We are never able to perform our real duties because real motives are never presented which would show us a true path where the present is more important than the future, the visible more important than the invisible, and the known more important than the unknown. We became wicked because everything taught us that we must be that way in order to be happy, after which we sighed.

So, the sum of human misery grows due to our superstitions, our governments, our education, our opinions, and the institutions we accept with the belief they will make life more pleasant. Most people are influenced by many, if not all, of the aforementioned flaws simultaneously, which is why so many people are so very confused. It cannot be repeated too frequently, *it is in error that we will find the true spring of those evils with which the human race is afflicted*. It is not nature that makes us miserable. It is not an irritated Divinity who wants us to live in tears. It is not heredity that causes us to be wicked.

It is error, long cherished consecrated error, error which is part of our very existence, to which these terrible effects can be attributed.

All humans are diseased, most from birth, when error contaminates the thought process. All are affected differently as a consequence of their natural organization. Is there a universal remedy which will indiscriminately cure our diseases? There is without doubt only ONE and it is TRUTH which must be drawn from Nature.

Despite the errors which blind the human race and the extravagance of our superstitions, not to mention the foolishness of our political institutions and our concerns about post-life destiny, there are happy individuals on earth. Occasionally there are leaders who are animated by the noble passion of making their citizens happy and seeing their nations flourish. Such people have elevated minds, placing their glory in encouraging goodness, finding happiness in controlling poverty, and think that supporting virtue is honorable. They recognize that the genius, whose contributions are timeless, deserves the eulogies of posterity and the admiration of fellow-citizens.

Of course, no government can make its entire population happy but it can and should be dedicated to serving the real needs of the majority. A society is as happy as it can be whenever a greater number of its people are fed, clothed, and housed. That is, they can, without an excess of work, provide the wants that nature has made necessary for their existence. Their minds are contented when they know that no power will take from them the fruits of their labor, that they are working for themselves, and that they sweat for the immediate welfare of their families. Unfortunately, there are whole nations where the masses are forced to work, wasting their strength and drenching the earth with their tears in order to maintain the luxury, gratify the whims, and support the corruption of a small number of irrational and useless beings. For this select few happiness has become impossible because their bewildered imaginations no longer know any bounds. This is how superstition and political errors have changed the fair face of nature into a valley of tears.

Because so many people cling to life, it cannot be concluded that we are unhappy. It is an exaggerated view of the evils of mankind that convince us that there is no remedy. Disasters will diminish in proportion to the number of errors we can eliminate from our collective thinking. We must stop thinking that because we continuously form new desires, many of which are difficult or impossible to fulfill, we are infected. As long as we require daily nourishment we should conclude that the body is sound and fulfilling its functions. As long as we have desires the proper deduction should be that the mind is maintaining a necessary amount of activity. From all this we should know that our passions are essential to the happiness of beings who feel, indispensable to those who think, and required to furnish us with ideas. Indeed, they are vital to a creature that must necessarily love and desire the things that contribute to comfort and promise a mode of existence that matches ones energies. As long as we live and have vitality the soul desires. As long as we desire we experience activity which is necessary. As long as we remain active we continue to live. Human life may be compared to a river where waters meet and push each other forward, flowing on without interruption. The waters must flow over a bed that is not of their choosing, encountering obstacles that prevent stagnation. It never stops undulating and sometimes recoils; only to rush forward again continuing with more or less velocity until it is restored to the ocean of nature.

Chapter IX

REMEDIES & RECAPITULATION

Whenever we fail to use experiences as a guide we fall into error. Our errors become even more dangerous, assuming a more determined corruption, when they are clothed with the sanction of superstition. At this point we hardly ever return to the paths of truth. We believe ourselves to be deeply interested in ignoring those things that nature puts before us, and fancy the idea that it is to our advantage to not try to understand ourselves. We think that in the interest of our happiness we must shut our eyes to truth. Most moral philosophers have been wrong about the essence of humanity because they deceived themselves about its diseases, they miscalculated suitable cures, and they administered ineffective or even dangerous remedies. All because they have abandoned nature by resisting experience, not consulting reason and ignoring the evidence of their senses. Instead, they followed the impulses of their imaginations which left them either dazzled by enthusiasm or disturbed by fear. Why were they so easily misled? It is so because they preferred the illusions that were believed instead of the realities of nature, *which never deceives.*

An intelligent being is always working toward conservation, real or fictitious interests, and permanent or fleeting welfare. In

36

other words, we are always working toward what we perceive to be our happiness. We fail to understand that desires are natural and passions essential, and that both are necessary emotions that feed the soul. Instead we suppose supernatural causes due to our lack of understanding and try to fix our evils with either useless or dangerous remedies. In an attempt to suppress desires, combat inclinations, and annihilate passions, our spiritual leaders give us useless instructions that are both vague and unrealistic. These vain lessons have influenced no one. At most they have restrained a few timid mortals who are not inclined to evil. More likely they have terrorized those who are more moderate in their nature, and never had any influence over those who are strongly controlled by their passions or habits. The promises of superstition and its dangers creates fanatics and enthusiast, who themselves are either useless or dangerous to society. It never makes us truly virtuous, that is to say, useful to our fellow creatures.

If we were to examine, without prejudice, the principles taught by superstition we would see that they were given to us by mortals who say the source is supernatural. As such, their fanatical dogmas are presented as fact. With the slightest reflection it would be obvious that these principles are as ridiculous as they are impossible to put into practice. To prohibit passions is to tell us that we cannot be human creatures. To tell a person with an active imagination to moderate desires is to require a change in temperament. To tell us to renounce our habits is like telling a man who is used to wearing clothes that he must walk around naked. So, superstition plunges us into misery, creating a violent inner struggle with the heart where there can be no winner.

Since passions are the true counterbalance to passions, there should be no attempt to destroy them. Instead they should be directed so there is a balance between prejudicial and useful passions.

Reason, the fruit of experience, is the art of choosing the passions that will lead to each individual's unique form of happiness. *Education* is the art of distributing proper methods of cultivating advantageous passions in our hearts. *Legislation* is the art of restraining dangerous passions while exciting those which may be conducive to public welfare. *Superstition* is the miserable art of planting unproductive labor by nourishing the soul with chimeras, illusions, impostures, and uncertainties, from which passions arise that are fatal to all who fall victim to them. It is only by facing superstitions with fortitude that one can place ones-self on the road to happiness. *True religion is the art of advocating for truth, renouncing error, contemplating reality, drawing wisdom from experience, and cultivating nature to our happiness by teaching the importance of helping others.* It is *reason, education,* and *legislation* that work together to improve human existence by causing our passions to flow in a current, gently creating personal happiness.

Conclusion

From everything that has been said up to this point, it is clear that the errors of mankind, whatever they may be, arise because we ignore reason, experience, and the evidence the senses provide. Instead we allow our misguided imaginations and suspicious authority figures to direct us. We will never find true happiness as long as we refuse to study nature and her laws. We must look to her alone for solutions to the evils that result from so many errors. We will be a mystery to ourselves as long as we ignore the laws of nature and believe ourselves to be two beings, one of which is moved by an inconceivable spiritual power. If we do not see our moral and intellectual faculties in the same way we see our physical qualities, they will always be a mystery. We must recognize that they are governed by the same regulations and submit to the same impulses as everything in nature. The idea that we are a free agent is contradicted at every instant by experience which proves that all our actions are necessary. This truth, far from being dangerous and destructive to our morals, gives us the insight to see why relationships must exist between sensible beings within a society. People congregate with a view of uniting their efforts for the happiness of all. From these necessary relationships come the duties that must be performed to coexist. As such, we will learn the sentiment of love which should be associated with virtuous conduct, while rejecting all that is vicious and criminal. All this will make the true foundation of *Moral Obligation* obvious, which is figuring out how to get what we want the most as a result of uniting in society. Each individual can tend to personal interests, happiness, and security by contributing to the needs, happiness, and preservation of associates and the community. It's about the necessary actions and re-actions of the human will on the necessary attraction and repulsion of our soul, upon which all our morals are grounded. It's the harmony of the will and the performance of our actions that maintains society. It is made miserable by conflicts and dissolved through a lack of unity.

From all that has been said, it can be concluded that the many names we have given to the concealed causes acting in nature, and their various effects, are never more than *necessity* considered under different points of view. It must also be acknowledged that the original cause, the great *Cause of Causes*, God or whatever you call it, is something of which we will always be ignorant. What we call *order* is a necessary consequences of causes and effects that we understand, or think we understand, and that we find pleasing and conformable to our existence. Similarly what we call *confusion* is a consequence of necessary causes and effects, which we do not understand and therefore view as unfavorable or unsuitable. A few other ideas we have designated are:

Intelligence – our ability to understand necessary causes that necessarily operate the chain of events which we call *order*.

Divinity – those invisible causes which act in nature according to immutable and necessary laws.

Destiny or *fatality* – the necessary connection between unknown causes and effects seen in the world.

Chance – those effects which we are not able to foresee or which we are ignorant of the necessary connection with their causes.

Intellectual and *moral faculties* – those effects and those changes necessary to an organized being whom we think is moved by an inconceivable agent and who we believe is distinguished from the body.

It has a nature totally different from the body which we call the SOUL. We believe this agent is immortal unlike the body. It has been shown that the marvelous doctrine of another life is based on gratuitous beliefs, contradicted by reflection, unsupported by experience, and may or may not be true. Mortals know nothing about the subject. It has been proven that the hypothesis of another life is not only useless to our morals, but it is calculated to stop us from actively pursuing the road to true happiness. Instead it fills us with romantic ideas that inebriate us with opinions that work against our tranquility. It takes the focus of legislators away from education, institutions, and the laws of society, all of which should be their true interests and duties.

Mankind! Listen to the morals which are based on experience and grounded on the necessity of things. Ignore superstitions that are founded on musings, deception, and the unpredictable whims of disordered imaginations. Instead, follow the lessons of those humane and gentle morals which conduct us to virtue through the voice of happiness. Turn a deaf ear to the useless cries of superstition which really make us unhappy, while making truth hateful and painting veracity in hideous colors, never leading us to respect VIRTUE. See if REASON, without the assistance of a rival who prohibits its use, will conduct us toward that great end.

41

O mortal, stop allowing yourself to be disturbed by illusions and phantoms that were created by your own imagination or that of some cunning imposture. Renounce your vague hopes and disengage from your overwhelming fears so you can follow with confidence the necessary routine that nature has marked out for you. Cover your path with flowers if destiny permits and remove the thorns that cover it if you can. Don't attempt to focus your views on a murky future whose obscurity ought to be enough to prove that it is either dangerous or useless to try to understand. Concentrate on making yourself happy in your existence. Be moderate and reasonable when it comes to your self-preservation. Balance your pleasures and avoid anything that can be harmful to you or others. Be truly intelligent by learning self-esteem so that you can preserve yourself and reach your highest goals at every moment of your existence. Be virtuous in order to make yourself solidly happy so that you can secure the esteem, enjoy the affections, and benefit from the assistance of those who surround you, which are those beings that nature has made necessary to your existence and happiness. And even when those who surround you are unjust, make yourself worthy of their admiration and your own self-love and you will live a content, serene, and remorse free life. For you, death will be a door to a new existence, a new order that you will be submitted to which is controlled by the eternal laws of nature, which maintains that to LIVE HAPPY HERE, YOU MUST MAKE OTHERS HAPPY. Allow yourself to be drawn gently along your journey until you return to that peaceable sleep on the bosom that gave birth to you. And if, contrary to my expectations, there is another life of eternal happiness you will surely be allowed to partake.

We must find and implement Nature-based solutions to all of the aforementioned societal problems. What will it take? The non-violent solution is to elect officials who are progressive and will fight for change. **To implement the necessary changes that have been discussed we must start by adopting nature-based solution in the areas of legislation and education.** *It's an uphill battle to change so many of these issues but change must start somewhere. We must find and support progressive politicians who are committed to working toward making our country and the world a better place to live. The two-party system will never give us meaningful choices that will lead to necessary changes. I've decided that I will not hold my nose and vote. Is there a candidate whose platform is a summary of this book? Truly progressive candidates get pushed out by the DNC, one part of the two-party system controlled by the wealthy and the corporations. Progressives who are catalysts for change are their greatest fear. When progressives run for office the elite see their power threatened and spend lots of money to maintain the status quo. Now is the time that we the people must come out in large numbers like we never have before to get people who will represent us in office and start making changes that will benefit our reformed Nature-based society.*

I have voted for Green Party candidates in the last two presidential elections. This is the party that provides a platform for which I can stand. For those who say I'm wasting a vote and helping one side or the other get elected, I say that I am voting against a two-party system and for hope. Hope that a majority of people, who are capable of change, will stand behind their convictions and vote for a society that works for, and represents, all its members.

*Joe Biden won the 2020 presidential election and has been sworn in as the 46th President of the United States. In the past he has supported big money and corporate interests such as war, oil and Wall Street, to mention a few, while ignoring the needs of the poor and the middle class. Can he change? Will he change? Now is the time for **we the people**,* *the voters who put him into office, to organize and try to influence his decisions regarding his Cabinet, Climate Change, the Corona Virus, Poverty, Endless War and so much more!*

THE

END

www.ingramcontent.com/pod-product-compliance
Lightning Source LLC
Chambersburg PA
CBHW030303030426
42336CB00009B/506